MW01533365

*To di*
*It is such a*
*pleasure*
*knowing y...*
*and having y...*
*as a frien[d]*

# Your Signature Style
## Unlocking the Confidence, Style & Influence of the Savvy CEO

ALICIA COURI

Cover Photo by Umbrella Syndicate.

Published by YourBook123.com

ISBN: 0692635904

ISBN-13: 978-0692635902

# DEDICATION

To my Mother Lena, who always pushed me to grow.

To my father Francis, who despite me not always understanding it, supported me at every turn.

To my siblings Leisel & Dexter for their wacky sense of humor.

To my Husband Duane, who has shown me unconditional love, support, belief in me and forgiveness.

To my Children Cassandra, Brooke & Elijah who challenge me to be better every day in every way.

To my Lord and Savior Jesus Christ, who saved me, delivered me, redeemed my life from destruction, who taught me how to love and value myself the way He values and loves me and created me to be beautiful!

# CONTENTS

## ACKNOWLEDGMENTS

To all my coaches and mentors who, for the last few years have helped me discover and unleash the real me so I can fulfill my purpose to help others do the same.

# Chapter 1
# Introduction

Growing up believing nothing about me was right has made my goal in life to put myself out of business.

Surprising? Confusing? Not quite sure how one thing leads to the other? Let's start at the beginning and I'll walk you through how I got from "I'll never look right" to "Not only can I look amazing and feel amazing, but I can help other people do it too!"

It's funny the things that stick with you as a child and shape the way you come to think of yourself. We all have these memories, including me; memories of things that other people would probably think of as unimportant or insignificant. For me it was the idea that being different was not good, that different was defective so if I was different, I was not good, not beautiful, and not acceptable.

At around four years old, my mother struggled with my hair, at least that's how I remembered it. She would put it in ponytail and five minutes later it was just an enormous unruly mess. Come to think of it, that's probably why I keep it straight today - "I'm going to tame you, hair, whether you want it or not." Anyway, my mom was just baffled by what to do with my hair at that point so she cut it all off! People started to confuse me for a boy, one of my uncles started calling me "Bald Head" which he continued to call me even as an adult; I believe that was when the seed was planted. That shift in how people reacted to me taught me that I was not cute anymore – I just looked like a boy - and taught me the importance of looking the part in order to gain the acceptance and approval of others.

As I got older I drew closer to my brother than I was with my sister. Although the age gaps between my sister brother and I are the same (3 years apart give or take a few months) I was much closer to my younger brother than my older sister, plus I was more of a tomboy. I was very much into playing outside and running wild with my brother. As a young teenager I was a late bloomer who got teased all the time about "not being a woman" yet. I remember going into high school where all of the other girls were already wearing bras and I just didn't have to, I hadn't developed at that point. I absolutely remember being so jealous that the other girls got to wear bras, thinking back on it now I have to laugh because when I started to develop, boy did I develop.

What really solidified my belief that I was not beautiful, and that everything about me was all wrong happened in Kindergarten when our family lived in Brisbane, Australia. I was one of only three black children in our entire school, and my sister was one of the others - there was one other but she was a native aborigine and wasn't as dark as I was. My hair was different, my skin tone was different. I would walk into a room and everyone would stare at me. Feeling the weight of people's eyes always made me wonder what they were staring at and made me feel incredibly uncomfortable. So I would always try to hide or to not be noticed because, in my mind, I was always noticed for the wrong things. I didn't feel like a typical girl, so I spent my developing years trying to disappear. It got to the point where I was so good at it that I truly did think of myself that way. I developed this "Invisible Woman Complex" where I was so convinced that people were ignoring me that I was almost incapable of seeing the attention they paid me even if it was blatant and in my face!

It was most obvious when I first met my husband. It took me a while to realize he was even looking at me. We were all on the dance floor, I looked over and I saw him looking my way, I assumed he was looking at the other girls who were dancing around me. In my mind I was convinced he couldn't possibly be paying attention to me. I still struggle with that sometimes, my mental default is still sometimes that I was and am invisible.

## To Move Forward, Go Back

So how did I go from wanting to be invisible to helping myself and other women own and optimize their feminine strength through beauty and style? Another question I have to go back to my childhood to start answering. I'm going to start by reminding you all that life is full of contradictions, and so are people themselves. While I was busy trying my best to be invisible, I was also soaking up every bit of beauty, style and makeup knowledge I could. I remember as a kid I wanted a Barbie doll so I could comb and style her hair. I never got that Barbie that I wanted, but I ended up getting something a little bit better. Eventually my mother would sit in front of me and allow me to style her hair! I started practicing on my mom and she would sit in front of me for hours because she loved having hands play in her hair. We bonded and my confidence in what I was doing really started to build. In a way, those sessions when I was nine years old were my first client consultations. My mom was my first and most important client but it took a long time before it finally stuck that this was something I could do and had a gift for – "A gift" I honestly believe all of us have one or more.

Imagine this scenario, I had two young children and I thought what I wanted more than anything was to be a stay at home mom, but it wasn't. I felt antsy. I felt like I needed to do something in addition to being home with the kids. I wrestled with guilt over that, but I knew I needed more, I needed something to do that would allow me to be home with my daughters but also be productive and fulfilled. I sat with that thought for a while not really feeling like I was going anywhere with it until one Sunday morning I was sitting in church. We had a guest speaker who started talking to us about what you're gifted in and what your talents are and how you discover them if you're not sure what they are.

You see, speakers have this amazing ability to present you with the questions that have been right in front of your face the whole time, but you just hadn't stopped to think about. Skilled public speakers make you stop in your tracks and go "Oh. It's that simple? Why didn't I think of that?" So I'm sitting there at church listening to this speaker talk and thinking to myself

*"Alicia, you don't even know what to do with yourself right now. He's up there talking about gifts and talents being what you should be doing, but it's been so long since you did anything just for joy you don't even remember... you know you need to do something but how do you know WHAT to do?"*

And then, as if he could read my mind, that speaker made a point that hit me and hit me hard. He said that to find your talent and to find your joy and the thing that will move you forward, you have to go back. Go back before you had a mortgage to worry about or bills to pay, before you realized that being a "grown up" meant you had to make money, back to those things you did as a child or a teenager. Those things that you loved doing; things that you were obsessed with but had to suppress because it was time to "grow up" or because you needed money, the things you dismissed as childhood hobbies but that brought you joy are actually things that the speaker suggested we all take a second look at! He suggested we work at those things and hone that craft and figure out how to turn that into not just your joy, but your livelihood – your business!

I went straight home, hopped onto my computer and pulled up a search engine. I typed in three words – "hair, make-up and weddings" - and boom I got thousands of search results and I thought "my goodness there is a whole industry for this." Mind you, I had my hair and make-up done for my wedding and I guess I just never put two and two together because I didn't even think that this was an industry. I just went to a hair dresser and got my hair done and had someone come put on my make-up but just thought he was doing me a favor, I didn't actually put it together that this is an actual service that people do just for weddings. So I started doing some research on it and I found a company that was willing to train me. I flew to New York for a few days and received training for the beauty business. They operated like an agent for me once I came back home, so they would send me to different jobs. Eventually from doing that I started to build up my own business little by little. Eventually, I started to take this on myself and I decided to no longer be a part of the agency, but just focus on really building it myself. Years earlier I graduated with honors with my AA degree in Fashion Merchandising from International Fine Arts College and during that time gained some experience working with and as a wardrobe stylist. That knowledge and experience became the seed for what I am now sharing with all of you.

So with my knowledge and experience and degree I was

ready to just grab success by the horns, right?

Nope.

## "I should get married today!"

What's that old adage? "If at first you don't succeed, try try again"? Well let's just say I tried, tried some more, tried a few more times, changed my angle of attack, tried again, and a few more times just to be sure. Overnight success wasn't in the cards for me and I am so very grateful for that. Did you think you were the only one who had to try a hundred thousand times before things panned out for you? Oh not at all. I mentioned I was grateful that overnight success wasn't in the cards for me. Curious about why that is?

The first thing you should understand is that my goal has always been to uplift women and to help them see beauty in themselves in a way that they haven't seen before. I want every woman I meet to KNOW that she is beautiful - to recognize it, appreciate it and to build confidence from it. When I do a client's hair, makeup and wardrobe I make it a point to make sure I am bringing out each person's unique and individual amazingness. What I give them physically is a combination of their hair, their makeup and their wardrobe. What those simple changes can give a client on a mental and emotional level are so much more than simple clothes and mascara seem like they should add up to.

Not sure what I'm talking about? Let me tell you about a client who paid me one of the loveliest compliments I've ever been paid. I met with her at 6:15 - yes, A.M. as in 6:15 in the morning - to do her hair and make-up for a conference. She's a speaker (are you seeing a theme with me and speakers and just how much I respect them?) and is just so bright, she's truly stunning. I listened to her talk as I did her make-up and hair. In my mind I didn't really do much because it comes so easily for me to see what I need to do, especially when a client is just so naturally dazzling. That's the beautiful thing about making a business out of your natural gift. Hair and make-up for this client was no big deal for me because I could so clearly see who she truly is and how stellar she was. That didn't mean it was no big deal for her, though. It left her gushing with gratitude. She kept looking at herself in the mirror and beaming, saying "I look so good I should get married today or something, I have to do something more than just speak!" Seeing her so over the moon - seeing any client look in the mirror and finally see how beautiful they really are - that's what fulfils me. Not having been an overnight success means that I have had the time to really hone that skill set, to be able to see to the core of my clients and find the beauty that they may not have known was there and it means I have been fortunate enough to see over and over again just how powerfully transformative this can all be. It cemented for me that this is what I love and that this makes a difference for my clients.

They say if you love what you do, you'll do it for free. Well it's true, because I've done make-up and hair for free all over the place because I just love doing it. But that's not where I really want to focus. I really want to focus on helping women feel that "I should get married today" way whenever they want. I want to set my focus on teaching the tools and the skills women need so they can do that for themselves.

## Putting Myself Out of Business

Do I really think hair, makeup and wardrobe can change the world? In a way, yes. My main focus has always been women in business, someone who is an entrepreneur – coaches, authors and yes, speakers. I have found in networking for several years that there are a number of women who work from home. Often, they tend not to have a separate office, they have a home office and that's that. It's more efficient that way.

Working from home certainly has its perks. It allows so many of us to balance motherhood with being a professional woman. It also has its negatives. A lot of times those of us who work from home will work in pajamas or yoga pants because you're home all day and you can. At first for a lot of people there is incredible liberation and freedom in being able to just roll over and get to work without even brushing our teeth if we want to (Don't worry, I've never done that, but I certainly won't judge those of you who have!).

I spoke to a woman once who said her mother always taught her that when you wake up in the morning you make up your bed and you make up yourself. Her idea was that if you get yourself together for the day, even if you are working from home, it gets you mentally together for the day. I like the sentiment, but I will be the first to admit - I don't always do that. I just find it comfortable to jump into work right away after I exercise. Once I've finished my work out I just shower and get right to work. I don't bother with makeup and all that. Yes, you read that right. The makeup artist often doesn't bother with makeup. And you know what, that's perfectly OK.

The problem comes when you are in that routine for so long that when you have to go out, it becomes a challenge. When pajamas and yoga pants are your everyday wear it's easy to slip so far into "comfort" that you almost forget what proper dress code is. How many times have you found yourself looking at your wardrobe completely at a loss? I'm guilty of it myself. I will raise my hand and admit it. Yes, I have stared overwhelmed into my closet wondering if I ever even had a professional wardrobe or if I just imagined it all. I have stared at myself in the mirror wondering "Do I look professional? I don't feel professional. How do I feel like me in 'professional' attire?"

So many of you might coach in your pajamas or your yoga pants; so many of you speak with your clients on the telephone while you're sitting on the couch and you're comfortable. It's not at all uncommon that when women in that position have to go out and meet people, that confidence and comfort is lost. Sometimes we forget how to put that package together. For some of us, life has happened and maybe that package has changed a little (or a lot) from the last time we had to go out in public and put on a professional face.

What do I see these women do time and time again? They go back to what they have been told for years is "professional" attire. I see so many women show up at the events in what is essentially the same outfit. It's like a uniform. It's the same sheath dress, maybe a blazer and a skirt or slacks. They wear pearls, because pearls say "professional adult". It's all the same color palette - black or navy blue dress, slacks, blazer; a shirt that is some shade of white or blue or maybe a touch of red to show "power and confidence". Can those things look professional? Sure! A lot of times, though, women will put on this "uniform" because they are taught that it's what looks professional to someone else's mind. Truth is, it can make you look out-dated, frumpy and like you've lost the things that make you unique – those things that attracted your client base to you to begin with!

There is so much more you can do with your professional look! My number one rule, and one of the most important things I hope you as a reader take from this book is that you MUST be authentic to who you are. Your professional dress shouldn't just be putting the same "uniform" on that everyone else does because you are not everyone else! When you put clothes on, it should feed who you are. It should be an expression of who you are. When you are able to wear something that really clicks with your personality and who you are, I think it lets other people see and feel the real you and connect with you more easily. When your clothing reflects your personality I believe it draws people to you. Whether it's using color or texture or print, just remember that there's no rule book that says you have to wear the corporate "uniform" and look like a corporate drone when you're at an event. In fact, you might be better off if you don't.

How does embracing hair, makeup and a versatile wardrobe equate directly to growing your brand? How does it help you in business? One word: Confidence. When you have more confidence in yourself, in who you are, you tend to step out of your box a little bit more and go for the things you normally wouldn't. Having that confidence and being a bit bolder will help you to find that same level of comfort you have when you're speaking to your clients from home in your pajamas. Why? Because you are 100% sure and being authentically you in that moment; you're communicating well, sitting up straight and tall allowing people to be drawn to you. You become a magnet, and it's all because you shirked what was "expected" of you and chose to stay true to you!

I'd bet you're wondering how we move you from pajamas and messy hair or from the "corporate uniform" to proudly owning every little facet of your personality and finding a way to make you look on the outside the way you think and feel on the inside, aren't you? Honestly, it's really not that difficult. Remember how I mentioned earlier that some people have a knack for presenting things to you in a way that makes you question if it could really be that simple? I'm hoping that this book and any follow-up discussions we may have will leave you going "Oh. It really is that simple. I can do this!"

First things first, we face your fears and your past. Whatever those fears are, however they present themselves in your individual case, we need to face them, own them, and get rid of them. Maybe they won't all be conquered right away, and that's OK. Often it's enough to just say "yes, I'm afraid of this thing, but I'm going to own this fear as opposed to letting this fear own me." Discovering or uncovering those buried memories of the past that may be holding you back or contributing to those fears is an important step in moving forward.

Next, we work on identifying and owning your world. No, not the world – we're not megalomaniacs here. I mean taking little bumps outside of your comfort zone, meeting new people, taking some serious inventory of yourself, your connections, your habits and yes, your wardrobe; basically the world you occupy. Ask yourself if you're happy with it, if you can change it, if you can expand it, can you shift it in another direction? Maybe your world needs to be tightened up a bit. Are you spreading yourself too thin and expending energy in places and ways that are not good for you emotionally, mentally, physically or for your brand?

Finally, we are going to talk about how to acknowledge and accept your influence. This is where things get fun – and sometimes scary. Yep, I admitted it. Sometimes it can be scary to admit to yourself that you are in a position of influence. Would you look up to you? Do you represent you well? Do your actions live up to your message? Can you take your own advice? I'm going to raise my hand and be honest and say that sometimes my answer to that last one is a no. No, I'm not always great at taking my own advice, but I'm human and so are you (most likely, anyway. Haha!) and so we are all constant works-in-progress. This last step is where we figure out how to create your image, your signature style, your message and – hopefully, given some time – how to put me out of business by giving you everything you need to be your own cheerleader, image consultant, motivational speaker and more!

Buckle up and let's have some fun!

# Chapter 2
# Face Your Fears

I mentioned in the introduction that step one for us would be to face and own our fears. Welcome to step one! Don't get nervous. In the next few chapters I promise I'm not going to take the path a lot of reality shows do and instruct you to stick your hand in a box full of spiders to face your fears head on. First of all, I don't know where one would get a box of spiders. Secondly, I think the fears that professional women need to face are often much less tangible than spiders and so they might be a bit harder to identify.

Before we get into talking about your fears, though, I think first we should talk about the idea of success and what that looks like to you. For some of you, success will mean a certain number of dollars in your bank account. For others, it might be an ability to do something for someone – I watched a documentary once with a young man who said he would be successful only when he was able to pay off his parents' home or buy them a new one with no mortgage payments for them. Some of you might have an idea of success that is less concrete. Maybe you will feel successful if you know you are helping people. My suggestion for those of you with markers of success like "help people" is to find a way to quantify that for yourselves in a concrete way.

## Defining Your Success Fingerprint

When I was teaching my program for Artists to create their own Makeup Line, one of the big activities for my students was to define what they wanted their cosmetic line to be. It was important that they, like you, understand that you can't allow "the people" to define who you are for you. When everybody else is telling you that you should do something a particular way, remember to stop and ask if that way is in line with your goals. I did not set out to be Revlon or Mary Kay - even though people repeatedly tried to push me towards that end – and I strongly suggested my students don't try to be Revlon or Mary Kay either. Or rather, I ask them why they think that they should try to be like those lines. The answer I get almost 100% of the time is that those lines are successful. That is undeniably true but those lines got to that point of success because they were different from what was already available on the market – and you should be, too! Revlon and Mary Kay are successful but those lines already exist and trying to recreate them is only setting you up to try (and probably fail) at recreating someone else's success instead of reaching your own. By defining your success for yourself, you position yourself for achievement and not some perceived "failure" because you are not lining up with what someone else already is. Of course you're not lining up with their success, because you're reaching your own success and not someone else's.

The main point I want you to take away from this section is that nobody can define success for you. Your ideas of success will be as unique to you as your ideas of beautiful or your personality or your fingerprint. You have to look inside yourself and determine what is going to make you happy, what things will motivate you and whatever the outcome of that inner inventory is – THAT is your personal definition of success. Success is not what everyone else around you wants for you; it's what you truly want for yourself.

Maybe explaining what success looks like to me will help you to understand how very different it can be from one person to another. After all, there's a chance my idea of success doesn't look anything like your idea of success does. Overall, success for me is broken down into a few different aspects. When I take on a project, I like to stop and think about what criteria I need to meet in order to feel like I have been successful with it. Of course I want to make sure I help people, and I have to define that for myself on a case-by-case basis. I also want to make sure that the project is something that will help me grow and is something I can later use to help others. For me, if I achieve those things then I know the project was successful, regardless of whatever the financial outcome of it is. In my eyes, my personal success is not always financial. If I have learned something that I can take away from the project and can use to help someone else – that is what I see as success.

Does that mean that I have no need or desire for financial gain? Of course not; I said success was not always financial, not that it was never financial. Financial success for me is tied more to the idea of goals in that hitting that financial goal is a form of success. Setting goals and hitting them is success! Throughout the process of working on whatever project I am working on at the time, I always bear in mind my three questions:

*Did I learn something from it?*

*What can I take away from it?*

*What can I teach others from that process?*

So if I did not hit my financial goal, but those other three things were nailed then, to me, I was successful at that project. I don't ever walk away feeling like a failure, even if someone else would say "well, you failed at that." If I learn something and I have something to take away and something I can teach someone else, then I don't look at it as a failure for me. If it fits those criteria, then it matches up with my personal definition of success – my success fingerprint - and nothing that anyone else says to me about it is going to change that.

## The Fear Breakdown

How does fear come into play? Let's think first about how people respond to fear. Some sweat, some stutter, some emotionally shut down, there could be any number of responses to fear but the ones we touched on tend to be pretty negative. Almost everyone thinks of one of the common negative reactions when they think about fear. Know what reaction to fear is not very common? Perking up, feeling great and getting out there to tackle your day with a positive attitude! When was the last time you were terrified of something and still marched toward it legitimately chipper and bright eyed?

Generally speaking, fear makes people unsure, it makes them close up and shut down; it makes people self-conscious. Stepping outside of your comfort zone to get to learn new things or gain new experiences is incredibly important both in business and as a general life skill. Can you take that step when you are ruled by your fear?

No!

That is why it's so important to be able to not only figure out what your fears are, but also to own them and how you respond to them. How do we do that? Let's take a look at one of the most common and deeply felt fears the world over, the fear of rejection. There are millions of people who fear rejection, but have you ever stopped to think about why? Or what it is we are really afraid of? For me, that is a very important part of facing and owning your fears – the breakdown.

No, I don't mean a literal breakdown as in snapping mentally or emotionally. I mean breaking that fear down to smaller bits and really examining it. When I think of rejection I think about the whispers of other people saying things about me. I think about not living up to expectations – other peoples' expectations of me or my expectations of myself. I think about that awful feeling of not being enough or not being as good as I thought or hoped. I have had times that I've asked myself if maybe I'm not educated enough, or am I not giving enough; the worst for me is when I start to really question myself. I say I am one thing, but what if I'm not? What if I'm a fraud?

In a way, I think we all kind of know it, but I was reading an article not too long ago that described fear of rejection as being a fear that all of the worst things we ever thought about ourselves were true. In a way, being rejected is a confirmation that yes, we are unlovable or destined to be alone or unintelligent or ugly or whatever our particular inner mean-girl is saying to us. Fear taps into the parts of us that we aren't comfortable acknowledging or dealing with and then picks away at our confidence using those insecurities against us.

When you look at it that way, the fear isn't really about other people is it? The fear, like most fears that I've dealt with, is really about the way we see ourselves and our personal confidence. People tell me all the time that I give them a great sense of value. While I appreciate it, there are some things you should all know. Firstly, I don't give you any value, you all already had it! Secondly, I sometimes sit back and wonder if I am giving enough; have I given each client their money's worth and more? Have I learned from them? Have they learned from me? Even I sometimes struggle with a lack of confidence in what I'm doing and that directly impacts me, and my clients – you.

## Confidence is Key

How does a lack of confidence impact you from a business perspective? Well, it may make you hesitate to even take that first step of becoming a business or building a brand. It's easy to convince yourself that you have nothing of value to offer, nothing that anyone would actually want to pay for. It's easy to tell yourself that you just need to get a "real" job and work, save, pay into your 401k and do the same thing so many other people are doing.

Except you're not "so many other people" are you? No, not by a long shot. If you're reading this then, at least in some small way, you probably already suspect that you might not be cut out for that sort of work. Or maybe you've already taken that big bold first step and have established yourself as a brand. If that's the case let's quickly talk about one of the most common missteps that people make when in the early stages of branding themselves and how it relates to a lack of confidence.

It's time to talk about money. It's OK if reading that sentence just made you cringe. When it comes to charging for your product or services a lack of confidence or a fear that you are not good enough can sometimes drive you to feel compelled to "prove" yourself. All too often that can lead to practically giving away your product in an attempt to be sure you provide great customer service and great value. The problem there is that your concept of "great value" can sometimes be overkill for the money paid. Once you've already established with a client that they can get X amount of product/service for X amount of money, you're going to be pretty hard pressed to get them to pay more for it. So where does that put you if you've already given the world and charged them five dollars for it? It certainly doesn't leave you in a position to keep that person as a client in any kind of a sustainable way.

Without the confidence in yourself and what you have to offer, you may never reach a point where you are comfortable enough to price yourself properly. This can be especially true if your brand offers something that is not really a product. Let's assume that a pair of pants may cost you $15 to produce. You sell it for $60 and there you go, you have covered your cost and gained profit and your customer has something tangible to show for that $60 that they spent. That's a simple enough situation, but it's not the situation that many of you are going to find yourselves in. So many of you are artists, speakers, coaches or entrepreneurs that don't offer a physical item for sale. When that is the case, confidence and sure-footedness are paramount to you being able to price yourself appropriately.

When I say that confidence is paramount, I don't expect you to just be able to just read the last few paragraphs and go "eureka! I've got it!" and march out into the world to own it like royalty. These things take time and repetition. Like I said, I'm not immune to fears myself. What I do hope that you do is take a few steps to help work yourself through those fears.

## Awareness, Ownership and Overcoming

First things first, let's identify those fears and gain an awareness of what they are. I approach this step over and over again, sometimes several times a day. I personally believe that any time there is a negative emotion there is generally some kind of fear attached to it. So as I go through my day I find myself going "Wait, I feel something negative. What is making me feel that way? Is there an underlying fear being poked at by this?" It may seem silly at first, but after a few hundred (maybe thousand?) times, it becomes like second nature. Honestly, this has been one of those skills that I have carried with me from my business life and into my personal life.

I know I mentioned negative emotions previously, but I want to talk about negative or self-destructive behaviors as well since they are such a huge potential obstacle for you and, in fact, for almost everyone. More than any other self-destructive behavior, I see procrastination destroy or undermine people. I see it almost daily, in fact! It's ok to admit it, we almost all stall. From time to time it just happens but not very many people ever stop to examine what's behind it. When I do it personally, I've noticed that most of the time procrastination starts with a sense of nervousness or anxiety about something or a complete disinterest in it. That may not be the case for most of you since we are discussing procrastination as it applies to your own brand and I'd like to think you're all interested in yourselves.

However, when you find yourself procrastinating, ask yourself why. Don't just ask, but answer and be honest with yourself! That second part is important. You may find more often than not that your procrastination is your way of reacting to your fears. You might be feeling nervous that a customer may not like the outcome of your work and that is normal. Doubting your abilities to some degree is perfectly normal. There is, however, another possibility that we need to touch on. Have you ever felt a fear of your own success? On the surface it might seem almost crazy to be afraid of succeeding, but I'm here to tell you it's not. Fearing your own success kind of makes sense when you stop to think about it. Success can be scary; especially when it might fly in the face of things you were taught or shown in your younger years. Does your success mean that you might have increased responsibilities? If you succeed at this one thing, will people increase their expectations of you? What if you can't meet those new expectations? Would your success mean that you are good enough after all and that your inner mean-girl has been wrong all this time? What else could you have been wrong about? If you've been working towards a goal for a long time and you finally achieve it, what will you do with your time now? Do you even know how to be happy? When you look at things through that lens, it almost makes sense to procrastinate or hold yourself back.

Whatever the fear or fear-based behavior is, the next time it happens I want you to stop what you're doing and ask yourself some questions:

*What am I feeling?*

*Has anything just happened to cause me to feel this way?*

*Why am I feeling this?*

*Is this feeling coming from my past that I have not let go?*

Once you have gone over those four questions with yourself and answered them honestly, a lot of times you will find that's enough to shift your perspective, however sometimes you may need to keep digging until you are looking your actual fear squarely in the face. Welcome to total awareness of it.

Now that you're looking your fear right in the eye, it's time to own it. Fears are not something to ever be ashamed of. Everyone has fears and it is so important for us all to just admit it. Ownership tends to be either the easiest part of this process for a person or the part that is borderline impossible. Admitting that you have a fear can be as simple as just saying "yes, I am afraid of this thing but I am working to get past it" or it can be a complicated production. Thankfully you get to be the one to make that choice for yourself. So which is it going to be? Will you boldly and honestly own that fear you're face to face with or will you refuse to acknowledge it and keep letting it get in your way? Once you've gotten past ownership in whatever way you choose to, it's time to tackle overcoming that fear because "God has not given us a spirit of fear but of power, love and a sound mind" 2 Timothy 1:7. We have the power to overcome it. So for that, let's "kick it old school" and take a look at a phrase that was popular in the 1980s.

"Fake it till you make it" yes I said it! This phrase kind of fell out of favor, I think, because people began looking at it as lying. I have a different opinion on it, though. I think if you allow "fake it till you make it" to not be an outward show then you're on a much healthier track for yourself and your brand. Instead of thinking of "faking it till you make it" as meaning that you just lie, pad your resume or exaggerate your experience or involvement in things – think of "faking it till you make it" in terms of pushing yourself to do things even when you are scared. Remember, bravery isn't a lack of fear. Bravery is all about acting to solve the problem or reach the goal even though you're scared.

When you're scared of something, go out and do it anyway! You don't have to be great at it at first, that isn't the point. The point is just to do and keep doing. Pretty soon you'll overcome whatever the fear was. In a way, you're using that repetition and tricking your mind into doing something by faking a lack of fear until you've legitimately made it into fearlessness.

Professor Amy Cuddy of the Harvard Business School did a study on Power Posing and how in just 2 minutes it can raise your testosterone level, the bravery hormone, and lower your cortisol level, the stress hormone, to the point where you feel more powerful and in control. The same works for smiling, you can smile your way to happiness if you aren't feeling your best. These are all scientifically proven facts and they are also spiritual realities. In the bible it is referred to as "Calling things that be not as though they were." (Romans 4:17)

## *The POSES:*

 *Wonder Woman*

 *The Victor*

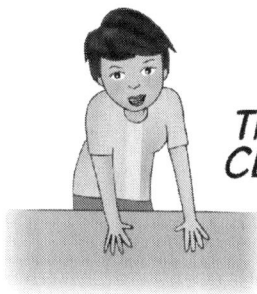 *The CEO*

 *The Star*

Another really effective tool you can use which some famous performers, and athletes use is the "Alter Ego Effect". I just absolutely love this technique. Think of the most extreme character you would like to play, someone who you could really step outside yourself and embody but still be very true to who you are. Beyoncé does this very effectively when she needs to perform onstage. She becomes Sasha Fierce! Sasha Fierce is not someone different to Beyoncé but an amped up fearless side of her that she lets out to play when she is onstage or at a photoshoot. Discover your alter ego and let her out and you see how much fun you can have creating this fearless side to you.

I saw a speaker some time ago who put the idea of fear into very clear perspective for me using a great analogy that I'm going to rework for you now. Think of yourself as running a race, only this race isn't on a typical oval track like you'd expect. Life is a bit more complicated than that. This race you're running is an endurance race, not a speed one, and it requires that the track be full of twists and turns and dead ends, just like life is. You need to be able to see all of your possible paths and options in order to be able to run this race well.

Imagine as you're running this race, you run into a fear that you struggle to be aware of, own and overcome. Fear tends to trigger the parts of our brains that are "fight or flight" and are programmed to look for one particular way out of a situation. What does that mean for you? It means that fear can very literally shut down your creativity and focuses all of your energy and ability to "see" only one particular path that may not always be the best way for you.

Have you ever had a fly buzz its way into your house so you open the door to let it back out but the fly just keeps flying and crashing into the one closed window, completely oblivious to another wide open and easier way out? Fear can turn you into that trapped house fly, making you fixate and obsess on only one possible way of handling something and leaving you incapable of seeing open viable alternatives. It works on people the way blinders work on race horses; only instead of narrowing your field of vision to help you focus on the finish line, fear narrows your field of vision to the point that you can't even see the track anymore.

Acknowledging and owning these fears and then facing them head on to help you overcome them is the only way to shake those blinders off so that you can see all of your possible paths – even some of the more unconventional ones - clearly again. This process happens over and over throughout the race of life. Don't think that because you've done it once or twice it will be smooth sailing from there on out. It won't. Just like any skill, though, the more you practice it the easier it gets. Get good at shaking off those blinders and pretty soon you'll be running an inspired, trailblazing race, forging paths where you didn't think there were any and making creative connections you just couldn't see through the fear.

# 10 Ways To Recognize
# You Are In Fear

*Awareness is the first step to overcoming fear.*

1. Are your <u>commonly held</u> beliefs not serving you?

2. Recognize when you <u>stop moving forward</u>.

3. What are you really afraid of?
   a. Success
   b. Failure
   c. What others think
   d. Self

4. Is your fear due to a <u>lack of information</u>?

5. Do you worry about being <u>wrong</u>?

6. Do you wonder if you give <u>enough value</u>?

7. When you experience <u>doubt and worry</u>, fear is typically the bi-product.

8. Signs you are in fear:
   a. <u>Procrastination</u>
   b. <u>Doubt</u>
   c. <u>Worry</u>
   d. <u>Making excuses for not moving forward</u>
   e. <u>Shiny object syndrome</u>

9. Unforgiveness is a great indicator that fear has somehow snuck in the door.

10. You find yourself very <u>emotional</u> over specific issues.

# Chapter 3
# Stepping Outside
# Your Comfort Zone

In Chapter 1, I mentioned how important it was to be able to step outside of your comfort zone for growth both on a personal and professional level. I think it's so important that I'd be willing to bet that most of your major successes and growth spurts have come on the heels of you stepping outside of your comfort zone and connecting with more people. I know how hard that can be for a lot of people and how just doing that, in and of itself, can be categorized as success. For others getting out there and talking to people is easy! For most of us, though, it depends on the day or the situation.

## Introverts and Extroverts

Before I really get into the nitty gritty of how to step outside of your comfort zone, we need to first talk about personality types as it relates to social interaction. Most of us have heard the terms "introvert" and "extrovert" and have identified as one or the other at some point. You have likely been taught that in order to be successful in the world of business you need to be an extrovert or at least take the "fake it till you make it route" and force yourself to be one.

We are taught that introverts are people whose motives, actions and activities are typically directed inward. Society tends to think of them as shy people who need to minimize the time they spend with other people and who are concerned mostly with spending time with themselves and their own thoughts or feelings. We are lead, then, to think of extroverts are people who are outgoing and talkative. The stereotypical idea of an extrovert is that person who is the class clown, the life of the party and can walk around with an easygoing smile chatting up anyone they want to. They are thought of as generally more friendly and concerned with other people than introverts are. When it comes to business, we're almost made to feel as if introverts are somehow less capable of leadership positions.

I'm going to challenge that.

First of all, I don't agree that people are either introverts or extroverts and that's it. I think of it more as a spectrum and people can move between the two based on the situations and where they are in their lives. If you are generally more reserved and keep to yourself, sure you may identify as an introvert. That doesn't mean that you can't or don't have moments where you are boisterous and outspoken and chatty with other people. If another person naturally tends to be open and friendly and comfortable approaching people or being around a lot of people, they might identify as an extrovert. That doesn't mean they don't sometimes need to just be by themselves to recharge or that they never get uncomfortable or shy. I identify myself as an "ambivert." An ambivert is someone who is both introverted and extroverted. For me in particular that means I can easily be that creative person who stays home comfortable and quiet, or I can be out in a crowd. It really depends on the situation I am called into. Do I sometimes want to be around people when I'm alone? Yes. Am I at times uncomfortable in large crowds and wish to be alone? Absolutely. However, being armed with the knowledge that I can have those tendencies, allows me to tap into what I need when I need it. I'd be willing to bet that's the case for quite a few of you readers as well.

## Work That Room

So how do each of the personality types learn to work a room and why is working a room even important? I'm going to start with the second half of that, actually. Make no mistake; learning to work a room is paramount for your business, especially if you are at an event. Talking to people, making connections, and approaching people are

ALICIA COURI

musts for building our brand. In the past, people at business events were almost expected to walk around, shake hands, exchange business cards, and trade a few pleasantries and move on to the next person. You know the kinds of events I mean; the ones where everyone is in a black or navy suit with the same shirt and nobody looks any different from anyone else and there's always that one person who tries to stand out from the pack by forcing too-loud a laugh at things that aren't that funny. Thankfully the times of doing business in that cookie-cutter kind of way are passing.

In fact, I actually don't like the whole business card thing. I've stopped carrying them myself and instead many times go to events with something of value to give, I learned that from one of my Mentors. When I go to an event, I make three to five meaningful connections and put their contact information directly into my phone with a text message so we both have a record of who we were and how we met. I began doing that because if you notice, after an event, most people just come home with a bunch of business cards and no idea what to do with them. Before certain software advents, people used to keep binders or indexes full of business cards, but now that's such an outdated way of maintaining your contacts. Let's assume you take those business cards home and add them to a contact list somewhere. Chances are, that contact list is going to be electronic and you're going to end up throwing those business cards away after you've added them. If you come home with a really big stack you might get overwhelmed, grab one or two cards from people who really stood out to you and just dump the rest in the trash or in a drawer somewhere without even bothering to add them

34

to any lists.

I'm not saying don't get business cards if you like using them, they are quite useful for giving to people here and there. What I'm saying is that using business cards to try and help you work a room just isn't as effective as it once was. Business cards at networking events should, in my opinion, only be given out after actual conversation and only when asked for. I think it makes a better impression (not to mention it's better for the environment) to have an electronic contact card that can be quickly dropped to a person's device. Also, your physical business cards don't have to be boring. Make an impression by making sure your card is as unique and individual as you are! There are all sorts of options like metal, clear plastic, cards that fold into interesting shapes, etc. I've even seen a business card for a florist that was meant to be planted and had wildflower seeds embedded into it. How creative is that? And what a wonderful way to drive home the message of who you are and what you're about! Remember, like we discussed in the last chapter, fear and any attempt to live by other peoples' standards can blind you to more effective, creative, and unexpected possible paths. Just because business cards are how it was done in the past doesn't mean it's how it has to be done now.

## Work That Look

I've said it before and I'll say it again, the standard business uniform of a black or navy suit or sheath dress is ridiculous and needs to be tossed out of a moving vehicle.

Dress like a classy and well put together version of yourself and people will be drawn to you. It doesn't matter what that is, I honestly don't believe there is anything you can't make work for your brand if it is authentic to who you are. Take for instance tattoos. Yes I'm going to go there. I was never a fan of tattoos because, personally, I don't believe in marking the body in any way. That is a strong part of my belief system so for me to suddenly get a tattoo would be in complete misalignment with my beliefs, and consequently my brand and people would know it. When things are visible and permanent, like a tattoo, understand there is a perception that goes along with it. Whether you like it or not, you will be judged by potential clients and 10, 15, 20 years from now it will still be a part of you, even if it's no longer a part of your beliefs. Don't follow after something that is popular or a fad because you want your success to have longevity.

Is your hair normally a bold color or texture? There is no law that says you have to dye it back to the color you were born with (if you even remember it) or wear it straight in order to be successful as a brand. There are tons of women who have built successful business empires without compromising their unique or edgy styles. In fact, in many cases, their success came when they embraced that aspect of themselves. Sure, lots of them are artists or performers like Katy Perry or Pink. But look at people like Kelly Osborne, Ursula Burns, Denice Torres or Jeannie Mai who have been able to break barriers and build empires while rocking brash bold color, their natural texture or even both! The only thing you need to look like in order to succeed as an entrepreneur is yourself. I'll say it again in another way.

Whatever you look like normally, keep looking like that, but let's amp it up so you are the best version of you. The person who goes to bed Sunday night shouldn't be a completely unrecognizable as themselves when they get to work Monday morning.

When you look and feel good – and like your authentic self - your posture is different, your smile is brighter, and your eyes twinkle. That's what I loved about the bridal work that I did. It was such an important day for my clients when they looked in that mirror and they knew they looked good; even though most of them were petrified of being the center of attention. So many of them said things like "oh I can't handle this, everybody is going to be looking at me" and I just say "well let's give them something great to look at." I think it can be the same at a business event! You may not be comfortable being the center of attention, but if you're going to be it, then you should be it looking great and looking like you!

When you're working these networking events and getting out of your comfort zone, you always want to be true to who you are. That not only means looking like you, it also means embracing the personality you have but pushing your boundaries. Like I said I am an introvert in an extrovert's body (Thanks Val Neighbors for that spot on description). I want to be true to who I am but have to recognize that in life and in business I can't hide. So, if you're naturally introverted that's fine and there are strengths to that, but you can't let yourself hide away.

My oldest daughter would stay in her room all day every

day if she had a refrigerator and microwave in her room. I honestly don't think she would ever come out if something didn't force her to. She likes to write, she wants to be a novelist. I tell her you can't live locked away and still be a novelist, you need people. I mean, what is she going to write about? The color of her walls? All of the adventures and relationships she could be having outside meeting people. When she took steps outside of her introversion she discovered she has a really amazing talent for media, both in front of the camera and behind the camera. She never would have discovered those talents had she stayed with only what was comfortable. Who's to say you might not discover really cool and interesting things about yourself if you give it a shot? When you're leaning too hard towards being an introvert, you need to push and make connections in order to grow.

I'm not just picking on introverts. Overly extroverted styles need to find some balance as well. Your quickness to approach and chatty nature can sometimes come across as salesy and overly aggressive. You may not mean to, but it does happen – especially when you're excited about what you're talking about. Nobody likes the "used car salesman" and nobody wants to accidentally come across that way.

The answer here is balance. Smile! I know everyone says it, but it really is a wonderful first step. Making eye contact briefly and smiling at a person is a wonderful way of saying "I'm approachable and not going to chew your head off if you try and speak to me" or "I might come and talk to you in a bit, but I'm cool enough to read your signals and go at your pace". In a networking situation, being able to send those messages nonverbally is beyond vital.

I challenge each of you to look at networking events a little differently next time you go to one. Believe it or not, I generally don't feel comfortable doing a booth at those types of events. Naturally I am not a fan of being in rooms full of people I don't know and just sort of standing there waiting for people to come talk to me. It feels awkward. I know I have to do it in order to grow my brand, but it's naturally not my comfort zone. What I started to do, and what I challenge each of you to do, is overcome that fear and really just interact with three people. Scan the room and sit next to someone you don't know. Resist the urge to immediately go to people that you know. Make yourself sit next to people you don't know and be the first to say hi and smile. Bonus: many times if you say hi and smile the other person will initiate the conversation so you won't have to be the initiator!

When it comes to networking tips, another helpful one is to never say "nice to meet you". I don't mean to be rude, I mean that we meet so many people it's possible to forget having met someone. Change the vocabulary from "nice to meet you" to "it's good to see you" or "how are you" and it will help you avoid hurting anyone's feelings if you've met before.

## Work That Sphere

Salesmanship 101: The people you know closest to you

are your immediate sphere of influence and most viable potential contacts to meet new clients through. Salesmanship 101 is full of all sorts of ideas that are just awful and awkward and uncomfortable for so many people – but that isn't one of them. I'm not suggesting by any means that you gather your friends and force them to sit through a sales pitch. It drives me batty when people do that. I'm saying that you don't need to be shy about casually letting your friends and family know what you do or see you in action doing it. (One of the best places for them to see you in action is on social media).

Some people refer to that group of people as your tier one or first level farm. I hate those phrases. These people are your friends and family, the people who care most about you and who you care most about. They're not radishes and pepper plants that you can just pick from. It doesn't work that way. I much prefer to think of them as a sphere of influence, and that's what I really want you to focus on doing.

Do not sell or market yourself or your product to these people.

Salesmanship 101 says these are the people you should be hitting up the hardest for your sales. I say these are the people you should never actively seek to sell to. Does that mean you can't do business with them? Absolutely not. If you do this correctly, you'll probably end up doing a huge amount of business with them directly or with contacts you make through them. What I want you to do with these people is to live your brand boldly around them. I don't mean talking about your company all the time.

Let's take a makeup artist for example. Around her immediate sphere of influence there is no need for her to talk about how much she charges for her time or what great new packages she has put together or any of that unless it comes up in natural conversation. Instead, I would suggest making sure her makeup is flawless and appropriate for whatever they are doing as often as possible and that's it. Maybe help them with their makeup a little bit here and there. I know sometimes it's more comfortable or immediately convenient to not bother being flawlessly made up around your closest friends who have probably seen you at your worst anyway. It's important to keep in mind, though, that when you are building yourself as a brand, in a way you are always "on" as long as you're around people. Just living your brand can bring in business.

Let me tell you a quick story about that. My pastor sometimes asks me to apply her makeup for her. On one particular time she asked if I could come in earlier to church before the service to do it. It wasn't something I talked about to anyone else; I was just living my brand. After one service in particular a friend came up to me and commented about how the pastor looked really good and how in their opinion, she looks more confident up there when I do her makeup. Very few people knew I would sometimes do that but, it was really interesting to me that something as small as makeup could noticeably increase the confidence of this already strong and dynamic woman.

Actually there are two really good lessons to take away

from that short little story. One, live your brand with your sphere of influence, don't sell your brand to your sphere of influence. Two, the way you look can change the way you feel and the way you feel can directly impact your performance. When it comes to stepping outside of your comfort zone to really own yourself, your brand, and your world there is nothing more important than the concept of confidence; confidence in yourself, your look, your mannerisms, your abilities and your skill set. You don't have to be perfect at everything. In fact, it's probably better if you're not. That might just come across as pretentious or intimidating. Just remember, this is your world and it's ok to make mistakes. Nobody runs this show but you. Nobody makes the rules but you. Nobody else in the world can give us what you do the way you do, so get out there and show us how it's done.

# 10 Point Checklist
# To Get Out Of Your Comfort Zone

1.  **High Power Posing** before an event for 2 minutes. Opportunity to Change your State.

2.  **Fake it till you make it** – This is an opportunity to create your alter ego. The fearless audacious version of you.

3.  **Preparation & Practice** – Being prepared helps you relax and the one way to be prepared is to practice.

4.  **Don't rationalize yourself out of opportunities**. Recognize your fear where your fear is coming from. Rationalizations is just another fear tool.

5.  **Have a strategy & plan of action** – Creating a plan to get you where you want to go is a sure way to keep you in motion.

6.  **Understanding your WHY** – Your why is the fuel that keeps your vehicle moving, without the right fuel you will sputter, stall or retreat.

7.  **Rehearse all the things that can go wrong** and find creative solutions – When you recognize you are in fear and resolve to do something about it you will be able to see a whole new world of opportunities and solutions.

8.  **The Detriment of the detriment** – Imagine what the world would be like if you didn't share your

gift with your ideal client. What would be the detriment to those people looking for you to help them? Then what would be the detriment of the result of that, and the detriment of the result of that? When you realize what you have and who you are here to serve has importance and value, you will get off your rear and go network and meet others, you will become the best version of you so you can serve at your highest level.

9.  **Evaluate your efforts** – Are you giving your all? Are you just being busy or are your being productive?

10. **Follow-up is King** – Most of my business was lost in the follow-up and that is where my biggest fear is. Don't lose clients because you don't follow up and follow through. Bring in tip #2, if you need help with phone calls, cold calls and follow up calls.

# Chapter 4
# Reach & Rock
# Your Red Carpet!

I mentioned that your sphere of influence was the most important group of people you needed by your side, but that it was important not to really to "sell" to them. When it comes to this group of people it's in your best interest to treat them not as potential sales, but as people whose lives you can have a direct impact on.

I'm not going to sit here and say that everyone is comfortable with the idea of having a sphere of influence. For a lot of people that word "influence" leans on some negative thoughts. It may make you feel like you need to be perfect in order to be a good example. I don't believe that.

In fact, I want you to try and wipe that idea from your mind right now, nobody needs that added pressure. All influence really means is that you have an ability to have some effect on a person's life. That's it. That's not so bad.

## Building Me

Some of you are spiritual, some of you may not be, but I'm going to explain how I learned to be more comfortable with the idea of my ability to influence people in a way that I understand best, which is through my relationship with God. If you are not a believer or standing in faith I urge you to open your heart to hear the "message" in what I'm saying. It's back-story time!

When I was in my late twenties I was searching. I didn't realize I was searching until I found what, or rather who, I was searching for. I walked through the doors of a church that felt like home the moment I stepped inside. Before then I was in a denomination, I always believed in God but never had a true relationship with Him, until I found that church, my church. I absolutely fell in love with learning more and more about the word of God, I was like a sponge soaking up as much as I could of the Word of God. Other churches had sort of just fed me the message as opposed to encouraging me to take an active role in my own journey. My Pastor not only talked about what's in the bible and how to read the bible, but encouraged me to ask questions, learn on my own and take personal stock in what messages I as an individual was getting from the passages. In that process - because it was in building that personal relationship with Christ - I gained a foundation for my confidence; because I had to realize who I was called to be as an individual. I wasn't worried about being a Christian or Anglican or Australian or woman or makeup artist or wife or mother, or any of those labels. This journey focused on Alicia.

I really had to understand that I was created for a purpose and that I am beautifully and wonderfully made. I came to understand that I am beautiful and it's not because of what I see and what I think, but because he created me to be beautiful. Until I started to recognize his work in me as a unique and individual person, I couldn't appreciate myself and I couldn't see beauty in myself the way I could in other people. A lot of times people would tell me when I was younger "oh you're so beautiful" but I couldn't accept it, I could not see that. It was so uncomfortable for me to hear that, because I didn't believe it. I mean even with my husband I was like "yeah you have to say that" that would always upset him because what I was saying didn't make sense to him. He was attracted to something, obviously, or we wouldn't be married.

Once I learned to accept and even embrace all of the little things that made me unique as an individual, I started to not see them as flaws or awkward quirks anymore. Even that extra bit of flesh hanging from my left ear was there for a reason and made me unique. I started to see all these things as perfect in their imperfection because they were ME and there was no other me in the world. So that was the big turnaround for me which boosted my confidence and started me on the path of seeing myself as beautiful.

I found my beauty and identity by discovering who I was created to be by the creator Himself. I encourage you, if you don't see absolute beauty when you look at yourself to find a way that is right for you to discover what I did. I need each and every one of you to start embracing the thought of yourself as an individual who is valuable and irreplaceable. There has never been another you before and there will never be another you again. The world needs you and needs your unique perspective.

**Building You**

Now that you know what went into my "aha" moment, I'm hoping some of you gave some thought to what your personal turning points were or could be. What is that thing that is going to trigger the change in you? What is it going to take for you to embrace the fullness of who you are while turning away from who you aren't and were never meant to be?

I'm going to stress that last bit again – it's time to turn away from who you are not and who you were never meant to be. Our families, society, our friends, our perceptions of what is appropriate, the media and just day-to-day life have a way of informing who we think we should be. When we're young children, we don't doubt who we are or what we're supposed to be doing. We don't doubt anything about who we are. We exist without fear. It's not until we get older and start trying to "fit in" that we lose that beautiful boldness of childhood.

Teens and twenties can be rough. We are bombarded with sometimes conflicting ideas about what's right, what's acceptable, what's expected, what's beautiful and what we are supposed to aspire to be. We're told to be smart, but not too smart or that might isolate people. We're told to be ambitious, but not too ambitious or we could miss out on a satisfying family life. We're told to be pretty, but not too pretty or we'll be seen as stupid. We're told to take care of our bodies, but not too much or we'll be seen as shallow.

The beautiful thing about our thirties, forties and older is that we start to tear down all of those things that we have built up that are sitting on a foundation of other people. Yes, it can feel awful and like things are being torn away from you, but there is also liberation in that. You've been torn down but now you get the joy of rebuilding yourself on your own terms and by your own rules.

How amazing is that?!?

How many times in your life have you daydreamed about running away and starting all over someplace else where nobody knew you so that you could totally reinvent who you are? You don't have to run away to do that. There's no reason you can't start tomorrow, or today, or even right now! Some people think of the late thirties to fifties as the "midlife crisis" stage. I like to think of it as the part of the show where we take an intermission and come back with a strong act 2.

This age seems to be about the time that women have their wake up call, their "come to Jesus" moment, their awareness that now it gets to be about them and that there's nothing wrong with that. Women of this age group are often in positions to be empowered enough to make their own decisions based on what they can do for themselves and by themselves. The strength and resilience and self-sufficiency of women at this age are a marvel.

So if you are feeling lost or down, confused or unsure, I want you not to worry. You have everything in you already that you need to rebuild. It's just a matter of knowing how to harness those things and to use them fearlessly. Instead of being discouraged by your age or your situation, take a step back and realize that once you've torn everything away you are completely free to build yourself any way you please. As long as you are still breathing, it's never too late to go after your dreams if you truly desire them!

## Ripe Fruit

As a younger woman I just couldn't see my beauty since I was too busy comparing myself to others and to what I thought society was telling me I had to be. As I got older I started to gain more of an appreciation for who I am and what I am, which I find is the case with a lot of women. It's funny because we tend to spend the years of our lives when society says we are the most physically beautiful feeling like trolls because we are too busy comparing to others. Comparison is the thief of joy. You are you and no one else, so the only person you should be comparing yourself to is the you that you have been. It's you versus you; there is no one else in this fight. If you've got a little age on you that's not only ok, that's wonderful.

Wine gets better with age; good fruit is only picked when it's ripe. Sure there are some farms that will pick their fruit before it's ready and had time to mature because they think its "more attractive" – now I don't know about you but I've never gotten a piece of fruit just to look at it and not eat it. To nourish a person's soul, to nourish yourself, to nourish the world in general you have to have something more to offer than just looking pretty. Beauty isn't just about tight skin and shiny hair. Beauty is about your wisdom, your experience, your intellect, your persona. Those things take time to develop and so I challenge you not to think of yourself as "too old" or "past your prime" but rather as fruit that is finally ripe and ready to nourish.

I want you all to be able to say boldly, honestly and without apology "I am beautiful". I went through a real struggle to be able to say those words and to own that idea. I had to find creative ways to force myself to own it and live it. I once heard a minister say that the 2 most powerful words in human language when put together are "I AM" because it's the very creative nature of God, so whatever comes after those words is what will be created. For me and my company I had t-shirts made which say "I am beauty" because that's what I am. That's who I am and that's what I bring. When I step into your space that's what's coming to you - beauty is coming. So when I wear the shirt, it empowers me, it lets people know who I am when I'm coming and that's what I'm doing; I just love wearing my shirts when I go to work.

I am now well into my forties, yes hard to imagine but it's true and when women hit their forties, their bodies change and we really start looking to find yourselves again. There is this beautiful thing about women in their late thirties and forties and older – they begin to accept that they don't have to be perfect little cookie-cutter fashion plates! That acceptance brings with it some of the most spellbinding and freeing power you can imagine. I think that's about the time that they stop looking for permission and they start really deciding "hey listen I need to make some decisions in my life" instead of going with the flow or going along or competing with everyone around them. There is a wake-up call around that age and they really want to – and are really ready to – make a change for full and complete ownership of themselves if they have not already done so.

It's my hope, honestly, that more women can come to that point earlier in life. I mean, just stop and think about that for a minute. If you realized your power at twenty years old and stopped buying into the things that people told you that you should be… wow. Just as one individual person your strength and self-assuredness could have an influence, an effect on, so many people around you. Can you imagine the world changing force women could be if we all stood up and just said "this is me; this is who I am and this is enough." Industries would crumble! Lives would be changed for the better! We women can really change the world, not just our personal world but the world in the greater sense. It has to start with us, though, and it has to start with us where we are right now.

For many of you readers that means it has to start with that 30something, 40something, 50something or

60something body. It has to begin with knowing how to handle that constantly changing body that you have now that might not even feel like you sometimes.

As a woman in that age bracket, speaking from a confidence stand point, if I am not happy when I look into the mirror or if I am not motivated to go out and meet people because I am not happy with my reflection, that affects my performance. I felt unhappy with my body recently; I wasn't feeling like the real me. When I sat my stomach hung over my pants, my thighs rubbed together and my clothes were really tight. Things had to change. It was only when I decided to invest in myself to do something about it, that in less than 30 days I totally transformed my body and have maintained it. Once you make a concrete decision to change, and get on the right plan, things can change for you rapidly but it all begins with the right mindset.

I know you've all felt this way before. You're not confident so you figure it's time for a new wardrobe, but because you're not feeling your absolute best, you don't know what clothes to put on. You lack the confidence to put yourself out there so you go back to what you know even though you are acutely aware that it's not working. So you end up going to whatever event just because you have to attend. You hand out your business card and don't really interact with anybody. You don't feel like yourself, you don't look like yourself; you don't stand out in the sea of other people. Once again lack of confidence and lack of a clear self-image is holding you back in business. All of that could be changed if only you had a better sense of your authentic self and how to present it.

It affects relationships, too. If you are a married woman, you might begin to worry that your spouse might start looking elsewhere because you've gotten frumpy, boring or old. What a self-fulfilling prophecy that thought pattern can become. If you are not looking or feeling great, then you are not able to give what your relationship needs. Because you are not giving your relationship what it needs and deserves, you inadvertently create distance which can lead to more insecurity and put you back at square one to start the cycle all over. I hear so many women say that after a certain time they just felt they had grown apart in their relationships. This doesn't necessarily have to be romantic; I've seen this happen in friendships as well.

How you have been feeling about yourself alters how you have interacted with your loved one. When you are not feeling beautiful or desirable or great about yourself, then no matter how fondly they feel about you, you subconsciously repel it. You push them away because all you can think of is the negative. So many times I have seen beautiful stellar breathtaking women shrug off compliments or turn away from people trying to connect with them because they feel so poorly about themselves that they just can't grasp that the desire for connection could be genuine. They deserve better. You deserve better in your romantic relationships, your friendships and in your business endeavors.

Confidence is the foundation for all of that "betterness." For instance, let's just think about the way you walk into a room. Ignore personality, whether you are extrovert or introvert etc. If you are not standing out, you are not as powerful as before. I, personally, have to push myself to go out to networking events because it is not something that is very comfortable for me. If you walk into that room confidently (even if you're faking it) you have a better chance not only of being more effective as a businesswoman but of being just plain comfortable! Let me be clear again, faking it doesn't mean being inauthentic, it means being afraid or uncomfortable and creating a persona that is you but a bolder you for others to interact with so that you can rise above that fear or discomfort.

There are people who will say they are too shy or introverts and unable to do it, but you can. You just have to be purposeful in doing it (Remember the Alter Ego). You can go out there and still be an introvert when you really look and feel good about yourself. People come to you. People want to know you. So when you walk into a room with confidence, people notice your energy and you don't even have to try and strike up a conversation with someone. Instead they will initiate it for you. I am an extrovert and I can be wild, crazy and let loose when I am comfortable in a situation. Yet, I am an introvert myself and I like to sit and observe people, see how they react and interact and stuff when I don't know anybody in a room. I can be up on stage, talk and mingle with people afterwards but if I let myself just go and sit in a room, I would literally just sit. I would not even talk to the person at the same table with me. How is that going to help me get anywhere in business? How is that going to help me just make my day less awkward? It's not.

## Rock the Red Carpet

I know this is all challenging. I know because I've done it. I've walked through the storms you are facing. I want to offer my hand to you all and help pull you through it. There are so many things you all have in store for your lives if you just manage to get enough confidence to own the fact that you do have influence and you can change your world.

When I teach women in beauty workshops or invite them into my Signature Style Palette Program workshop, I focus on empowering them to build their confidence by capturing, expressing and owning a "Style that is True to You that you Love and are Excited about". We work with three main concepts; beauty, image and influence to help you REACH your success goals!

What do I mean when I say "REACH"? I like to think that everyone has another self, a heroic, remarkable and powerful individual! Most people never get a chance to meet this person unless they experience an extreme challenge. There is however an opportunity to REACH this hero inside through conscious effort. My Signature Style Palette Program is designed to help you REACH your goals. I do this by breaking things down into five steps; REACH.

**R**: **Reframe your past to ignite your future**. I used to have a horrible habit of redirecting or quitting on myself when things got hard or scary. I know quite a few of you do as well. Once I recognized that I was sabotaging myself,

I took the time to reframe the memories and bad habits that were leading to the behavior that was stopping me from reaching my full brilliance and may be stopping you from reaching yours.

**E**: **Embrace the Truth about You**. Take a long look at yourself without sugar coating anything. Understanding who you are now deserves to be embraced and loved. But also being real with yourself allows you to fully embody your signature style. Your signature style is wrapped up in your uniqueness! You need every little flaw you think you have. You may change, sure, but who you are now is worthy and valid and should be encouraged.

**A**: **Alter Ego Effect**. Get that alter ego out and go play! You may be shy, you may be awkward, you may be uncomfortable, but your alter ego knows exactly what they're doing and has none of those hang ups. Create your superhero and hand them the reigns when you need to.

**C**: **Consistency is key to your success as an entrepreneur.** If you cannot be consistent, then you cannot develop a signature style or a brand voice. It's as simple as that.

**H**: **Have Fun!** I should hope you are open to this last step and have learned by now how very important the fine art of play is. Let's have some fun creating your Signature Style and getting you red carpet ready!

My program is all based around the concept of the Red Carpet CEO. When I look at celebrities or dignitaries on the red carpet, I think of 5 things: First they are important, second they are top of their field, the best of the best, third in high demand, forth they are influencers and fifth they are well put together from the hair and makeup to the dress nails shoes and accessories. No woman walks the red carpet totally shabby like they rolled out of bed, whether they are chic in real life or not. The Red Carpet CEO knows how to pull herself together for an important event or client even if your everyday wear is yoga pants or PJs.

Earlier I talked about the 3 major concepts of the Red Carpet CEO, Beauty, Image & Influence, let's skip over the first two and talk influence for a moment, because we already know you are great at what you do and you are a leader. How many times have you seen a dress or accessory or hairstyle on the red carpet only to have it start popping up all over the place in some way afterwards? There are best dressed and worst dressed lists everywhere. There are designers who make lines that are only pieces influenced by red carpet fashion. Red carpet interviews can give us sound bites that will be played over and over across various forms of media. That is the kind of influence I want my clients to have! When your confidence level is up and your energy shifts, you create influence without even trying.

One of the most simple and effective ways to teach you to embrace that as a possibility is with your look. You obviously don't have to be wearing a designer gown every time you walk out the door, but be purposeful with your look. I'd often walk out the door to go to a client for makeup & hair wearing jeans and my "I am beauty" t shirt. My hair and makeup will be done and my jeans and shirt fit well and it lets me be comfortable, show off who I am and give me that top-of-my-game confidence. It doesn't have to be complicated; it just has to be me. It doesn't have to be complicated; it just has to be you.

When it comes to beauty I am saddened by the statistic marketed by Dove Campaign for Real Beauty that says only 4% of women consider themselves as beautiful. That means an alarming 96% of women don't see beauty in themselves. I was one of those 96% until I decided to jump off that train and get on the 4% train. My greatest desire is for those statistics to flip flop so my lessons on beauty not only cover makeup, hair and skincare which is a lot of fun, but more importantly, the mindset of beauty; how to transform your thinking to accept yourself as beautiful. Self-care begins in the mind and then spreads to the outside. We talk about creating a signature style, how to dress to best represent your brand and be functional while working and 100% yourself.

For a lot of my clients, figuring out what works on their current body can be a challenge. A lot of people have weight loss or body recomposition goals and tell themselves they're not going to get any new clothing or really invest in how they look until they have hit those goals. Some have kids in college and still trying to lose that "baby weight". In the mean-time haven't updated their look.

I, personally, think that is one of the worst things you

can do for yourself.

First of all, you can't go everywhere in yoga pants or pajamas and still look and feel confident. You just can't, unless you are teaching a yoga class all day. You can't be naked all day long either (though some of your significant others might send me thank-you notes if you read this book and decide that's what you're going to do.) The body you have right now might not be the one you want, but it is the one that is housing that strong beautiful soul of yours and it deserves your respect. Maybe you've never been as thick as you are right now and you're not sure how to dress that frame. That's ok, that is something that can be taught and learned. Maybe you just came through a weight loss and you don't know what to do with your smaller self. That's ok, that can be learned too! There are styling and wardrobe tricks for just about everything. You deserve to show you a little bit of respect and dress you like you love you.

I'll tell you a little secret, something I drill into my clients in my Signature Style Palette course, looking your best isn't something you put off until you reach your goals. Looking good is something you do to help you reach your goals. When you look a mess, you feel a mess and I don't know very many people who can feel like a mess on a regular basis and still manage to be as authentic and wonderful and amazing as they could be. Sure, they may be absolutely stellar, but they could be so much more if they took the time to be good to themselves.

Your image, which we also cover, helps tie in not only how you are dressed but things like mannerisms and marketing materials and generally how to brand yourself together with your business. We talk about the importance of not dancing to the beat of anyone else's drum and not pretending that you don't have uniqueness to you. So many times we see the things that are special and wonderful about other people but just can't seem to turn that discerning eye inward. The image portion focuses on helping you make sure everything outside is a full reflection of what's going on inside.

I want to help you understand your bodies, how to incorporate color, fabric and style to suit your personality. Then I want you to take that understanding and apply it to the rest of your brand, your marketing materials, your message, everything.

Have you ever considered how choosing a brand color can affect your marketing? Color fills every aspect of our lives, but have you ever really taken the time to understand the psychology of color? Color is a powerful non-verbal tool that speaks volumes without saying a word. Color can be effectively used in your beauty, image and definitely influence. It instantly sets a mood, creates emotion and can inspire people to take action. Are you using the power of color effectively?

Another really exciting part of the Style Palette program is the opportunity to understand your value and your worth by exploring your Spiritual TAGs. Style is so much more than clothes and color, it is your essence and discovering your Talent, Assets and Gifts will be invaluable to you. I had so much trouble understanding and recognizing my own value that beginning to embrace this not only allowed my own self-worth blossom but also my beauty.

Becoming the top of mind in your industry is what being a Red Carpet CEO is about. So with that in mind finding opportunities to speak, get radio and television interviews is an opportunity to grow your influence. Showing up on social media as the go to person, especially when you are recommended by people you don't even know, is when you know you are impacting those around you. People love to see what you are up to and you serve as a way to encourage them to live a bigger life than they ever dreamed of doing just by watching you.

Having the power to reinvent yourself and nourish both yourself and your style is an opportunity to experience success, the decision is yours. One of my favorite books is Think and Grow Rich. In it Napoleon Hill says, "To grow, ideas need the breath of life injected into them through definite plans and action".

It's my goal to help teach you all how to do that with a definite plan that you can take action. To help you accept yourself as a beautiful woman in a position of influence!

# Chapter 5
# **Conclusion**

I think a lot of times, as women, we don't always see ourselves as potential world changers. There's a story of a father and son who were in a terrible car accident, they were rushed to the hospital and when they got there, the son, in critical condition, was raced into surgery. Upon arriving in the operating room, the chief of surgery looked at the boy and declared "I can't operate on this boy, he's my son!" So how can this be? It's a story about stereotypes.

We often think of doctors, lawyers, presidents, monarchs, military leaders and religious heads generally as men. The chief of surgery couldn't operate because she was his mother. Men are a small part of my clientele of course, I would never turn anyone away who needed me. However, to be honest the bulk of my clients and my main focus is women. My goal, and what I believe my purpose is, has always been to empower women.

All too often I feel like women are taught to view one another as competition as opposed to potential sisters, friends, confidantes and battle buddies. We view one another with suspicion or jealousy as opposed to genuine admiration. We tend to see other women and sometimes don't even fathom the great things they are capable of – and that we are capable of. Someone very close to me once pointed out that our history books are full of men who did great things and sometimes mention the women who helped, but very rarely talk about the women who did amazing things on their own. Unfortunately, this is especially true of women of color. I don't recall ever being taught about the Kandakes, queens who ruled the ancient Kush civilizations. I most certainly wasn't taught that it is believed one of them was so powerful a ruler and military strategist that Alexander the Great avoided her territory. Can you imagine that? A woman so strong that Alexander the Great (the man's name literally contains "the great") took a look at her might and went "well … let's just go the other way." I want us all to feel that powerful in our own worlds.

In order to do that we all need to be able to move beyond the road blocks that we set up for ourselves. Honestly, I truly believe that almost all of those road blocks just boil down to being about fear; fear of rejection, fear of failure, fear of success – just fear. Fear is a force of destruction in most of our lives, it makes us doubt and engage in self-destructive behaviors like procrastination or just plain giving up. Fear resides in our sub-conscious mind designed as part of our defense mechanism and is running at a speed of 400 billion bits per second, which means our reaction to fear is so imperceptible to our conscious mind that we live with it, make excuses for it and continue along agreeing with it, until... Until we decide to not put up with the results we have been experiencing and long for something more. It's funny, most of us don't think about procrastination as a fear based behavior but if you really dissect it, it's often something you do when you're wrestling with doubt or disinterest.

Moving past your fear isn't easy. It first requires you to acknowledge that the fear exists and that it's holding you back. Awareness is really the first step to change. By becoming aware of the symptom of fear, you have slowed down the sub-conscious reaction and actually slowed it down to the conscious level of 2000 bits per second and when that happens then you get to choose your reaction, it's no longer involuntary. You have the opportunity to decide your next move.

I remember one incident in particular that happened not too long ago in my career that I often tell my students about in my courses. I was in a training with my friend and mentor Kellie, she had someone come in to do image consulting with a group of us individual business owners that she was coaching. The consultant was wonderful and went through how to properly dress, the rules to keep in mind for our body types, the importance of sticking with a style that reflects our personality and more. I'd had years of fashion training so I knew all about what she was teaching. Finally, Kellie just turned and looked at me and asked "why do I have to bring someone else in? You know all of this stuff, why didn't you do it?"

The truth was that I didn't even think about it because I didn't feel confident going into it because I had done it so long ago. I had just decided that my experience wasn't relevant anymore because I lacked the sense of value in myself and what I knew. I let the opportunity pass without even trying out of a sense of fear, but as I sat there listening to the consultant talk everything came flooding back. As it turned out, I could have done it if I had believed in myself and tried. For over a decade at that point I had been working in the beauty industry but I had all of this styling and fashion training that I wasn't using. I decided I would marry one to the other and use that to help empower women.

In order for me to even believe I could do that, I first had to come to conscious awareness that I was in fact afraid and exactly what that fear was. Then I had to own it and admit yes, I was scared. Once I did that and I made up my mind to conquer that fear, the blinders came off and I was able to see all sorts of new potential connections I didn't even realize were there or think of as possible. I want that for you. I know you can have that "Ah ha!" moment where it all clicks and falls into place.

All you need to do is conquer that fear, embrace all of your fabulousness, look in the mirror, and take a deep breath and just say "yes." Yes, you are beautiful. Yes, you have value. Yes, you are enough. Yes, you have a purpose. Yes, you are afraid. Yes, that is OK. Yes, you can do something about it. Yes, you can make your own rules and run your own world. Yes, you deserve that. Yes, you are in a position of influence. Yes, that's ok too – not only is that ok, but it's needed. Yes, needed. Yes, we all need you and your ideas and your point of view. Yes, you're a force to be reckoned with. Yes, you deserve to rock your red carpet.

I imagine all of you as potential Red Carpet CEOs, like this is a movement – no, this is a revolution in womanhood! I imagine you all having boosted your beauty, increased your personal glam and slapped the frumpy and the boring right out of your image – not just the image you show others but, more importantly, the image you have of yourselves in your head. I feel like if we can all proudly embrace the truth of who we are and how amazing we are, the world will be ours to change for the better! When everything is said and done I want you all to be able to get up, get yourselves together and walk out the door ready to start treating the whole world as your personal red carpet. I would love nothing more than to be able to pass you in the street and feel the confidence radiating off of every woman I pass – including you - and think "wow, she is really rocking her red carpet today!"

And you will. You already do. You just don't know it yet.

ALICIA COURI

# Bonus:
# **Red Carpet CEO**
# **Essentials**

Baker's Dozen Red Carpet Checklist of Essentials. I love to give a little extra so instead of a dozen we give you a Baker's dozen. These are the essential items for style and beauty. Great to take shopping and to go through your closet to see what you have and what you might still need.

# Basic Essentials

1. Nude Heel
2. Tote
3. Scarf
4. Ballet Flat
5. Bold Trench
6. Body Shaper
7. Skinny Belt
8. Modern Pearls
9. Wrap Dress
10. Leggings
11. Chandlier Earrings
12. Diamond Studs
13. Clutch Purse

# Work Essentials

1. Crisp White/Beige Shirt
2. Navy Blazer
3. Menswear Pant
4. Twin Sweater Set
5. Black Skirt
6. Business Handbag (High quality bag to elevate your look. Hand stitched leather, pop of color.)
7. Black/Brown Pantsuit
8. Grey Flannel Suit
9. Black Pumps
10. Grey Pin Stripped Suit
11. Black Turtleneck
12. Simple Pearl Necklace
13. Basic Black Dress

# Night Out Essentials

1.   Party Dress
2.   Chic Low Heel
3.   Leather Jacket
4.   Sequined Tank Top
5.   Scarf Blouse
6.   Skinny Jeans
7.   Camisole
8.   Jaw Dropping Evening Dress
9.   Wide Belt
10.  Knee Boots
11.  Hoop Earrings
12.  Cocktail Ring
13.  Stylish Watch

# Weekend Essentials

1. Black Jean
2. Wedge Heel Sandal
3. Menswear Pinstripe Shirt
4. Khaki Trouser
5. Tote
6. Denim Jacket
7. Polo Shirt
8. Track Suite
9. White/Blue Jeans
10. Linen Shirt
11. Jean Shorts
12. Capris
13. Flip Flops

# Beauty Essentials

1. Cleanser
2. Serum
3. Moisturizer
4. Fragrance Atomizer
5. Gum/Mints/Breath Spray
6. Floss
7. Hand Lotion
8. Nail File
9. Nail Clipper
10. Comb/Brush
11. Wipes
12. Pads/Panty Shields/Tampon
13. Eye Drops

# Makeup Essentials

1. Perfect Red Lipstick
2. Concealer
3. Translucent Powder
4. Hydrating Lip Balm
5. Lip Gloss
6. Perfect Foundation
7. Mascara
8. Brow Kit
9. Eye Primer
10. Face Primer
11. Shadow Palette
12. Makeup Brushes
13. Eye Liner

# ABOUT THE AUTHOR
## ALICIA COURI

Alicia Couri, founder and president of Red Carpet CEO™ and creator of the Style Palette™ Program, is a speaker, author, international celebrity makeup artist and style expert. Alicia has appeared on ABC, CBS, NBC and a host of other media outlets and speaks on stages around the world.

Alicia's goal is to encourage female entrepreneurs to create their Signature so they can attract more clients and earn more money. She shares her story of overcoming low self-worth and poor self-esteem to standing in audacious courage that inspires others. Alicia believes "to whom much is given, much is required" and utilizes her experience and shares her wisdom with others to elevate them to their highest potential.

# What people are saying...

*Alicia Couri is brilliant. Her story is powerful and compelling because she is so relatable. She shares sound advice in a fun way, but what I really love is the way she lays out easy to follow action steps. She addresses different personality types, how to develop your inner confidence and how to be confident when interacting in groups. A complete masterpiece! Read this book and it will allow you to move confidently into a brighter future. Six out of five stars!* - Cassi Eubank CPC, CHt, NLP Rock Star RESULTS Coach

*"Never judge a book by it's cover! Alicia Couri knows firsthand the torment of other people seeing your beauty before you do. Her journey of healing has now become her passion to help others see how fearfully and wonderfully made they are from the inside out! Her gift of makeup artistry and entrepreneurial resourcefulness is a BONUS! Her story will change the way you define beautiful!"* - Dr. Vikki Johnson, CEO, Authentic Living Enterprises & Creator, Soul Wealth Academy www.vikkijohnson.com

*Alicia Couri takes a reader through her courageous journey of finding her inner beauty and power in the world. Alicia Couri is a powerhouse in the beauty and self-empowerment industry who boldly has assisted other women to find their truest expression of their style and 'mojo' in the ever developing world of cosmetics and fashion. Alicia's authenticity and dynamic insight about herself and the world will inspire any reader in their own journey of self-discovery. I worked personally with Alicia and her giving ways, coupled with her foresight for all details related to looking and feeling your best, made for the most fantastic work product.* - Pam Olsen, J.D., M.S.

*When I first met Alicia Couri I knew she was someone I wanted to have in my life. She has such style and grace, is honest and caring, a truly wonderful soul. You would never have a hint about her past insecurities if she didn't tell you, she has chosen to get past it all. She has grown and continues to grow to be the best person she can be.*

*In working with Alicia you get it all, she goes the extra mile to make sure you do it right. She gives it her all! I feel blessed to have her expertise, her wanting to help me be a better person, get my speaking going and teaching me how to be a Red Carpet CEO. I highly recommend working with Alicia Couri!* Margie Friedman

*Alicia Couri is the quintessential beautiful woman on the inside and out! It's no surprise that she's a leader in the beauty business. Alicia works on creating your beauty from the inside and brings it all out for the world to see beautifully. I have trusted Alicia for her wise advice and expertise in branding and creating a powerful memorable image, and I highly recommend her services to anyone that needs to create a great branded image for themselves and their business.* - Vicky Townsend Inspiration University & W.I.N.G.- Women Influencers Network Group.

*Alicia Couri writes from an extensive background of achievement and knowledge to present a book of techniques that share the importance of being who you are at all levels. Beauty is an inner game.* Karen Alleyne-Means, Intuitive Business & Empowerment Coach www.KarenAlleyneMeans.com

*Alicia Couri is a unique gem with an innate ability to express her vast knowledge and expertise almost as though she is speaking directly to you throughout the book. She has the unique manner to enable the reader to connect their own experiences whilst being guided by her astute 'know how' to step into being beautiful both inside and out and realizing the power of inherently claiming your CEO style!'*
- Raj Anderson - Savvy Strategist for the Enlightened Entrepreneur

*The very first time I met Alicia Couri, I was in the market for a headshot and I was in a dilemma over what would reflect my authentic style. Alicia listened thoroughly as I proceeded to describe my thoughts at length. After careful consideration, she suggested that I try both to see what looked best on camera, and she recommended a photographer who she worked with before who would be willing to "play around" with wardrobe changes. It occurred to me that Alicia had just found a solution that gave me 100% ownership of my own authentic style. I could consult with her as a stylist, and the photographer, and then decide for myself what looked best on camera. I hired her on the spot.*

*What I know about Alicia is she is committed to women owning their own beauty and style in a way that enhances their whole life. Alicia has an elegance and grace about her that inspires everyone she meets to tap into their own authentic beauty.* - Jane Cabrera / JaneCabrera.com

*There is no one on the planet more qualified in helping women become Red Carpet Ready than Alicia Couri. As a professional speaker and global businesswoman, I have grown in my confidence and ability to own my style and the stage thanks to the wisdom of Alicia Couri!*
– Kellie Kuecha, CEO of Kellie Kuecha World Enterprises

*Alicia's book is of courage and inspiration. She puts a new twist on confidence by leveraging your personal style. It really is about leveraging our image, and beauty to boost our self-esteem and branding. The book is so much more than just your appearance on the outside and Alicia's book is one of confidence needed to win in life and business. It is a must read.* - Val Neighbors, The 7 Figure Introvert

*I met Alicia Couri 3 years ago at an event where I was the photographer and she was the stylist/makeup artist for the keynote speaker. Time and time again after that, I would see her at the same events. I quickly saw the benefits of working with Alicia as someone whose work I know, like and trust and we took the opportunity to recommend each other's services. It's funny reading the book because I was the photographer that day when she referenced the client/speaker who wanted to get married because she looked and felt so amazing. Alicia truly has the business savvy to go along with a great sense of style. My job as a photographer is much easier when Alicia has been the stylist/makeup artist because she puts the clients at ease by listening to them and encouraging them to explore different options before they make the final decision.*

*Alicia is a pleasure to work with. Just knowing that she is a part of the team brings a level of confidence and professionalism to any project.*
CeCe Espeut / CeCeThePhotographer.com

45626595R00052

Made in the USA
Middletown, DE
09 July 2017